T0287891

In a

January

Would

In a January Would

poems

Lonely Christopher

Roof Books
New York

ISBN: 978-1-931824-85-9

Library of Congress Control Number: 2019957194

Cover image by Gustave Courbet, *Fox in the Snow,* 1860

Interior Design by Virgil B/G Taylor

Author Portrait by Rijard Bergeron

NATIONAL ENDOWMENT for the ARTS
arts.gov

This project is supported in part by an award from the National Endowment for the Arts.

NEW YORK STATE OF OPPORTUNITY. | Council on the Arts

This book is made possible, in part, by the New York State Council on the Arts with the support of Governor Andrew Cuomo and the New York State Legislature.

Roof Books
are published by
Segue Foundation
300 Bowery
New York, NY 10012
seguefoundation.com

Roof Books
are distributed by
Small Press Distribution
1341 Seventh Street
Berkeley, CA. 94710-1403

I could liken you to a werewolf the way you left me for dead
But I admit that I provided a full moon.

Fiona Apple

The Order

In a January Would

I rode a bike past your house so many times I forgot who lived there
first through the rough tranche of midsummer
only later, less impervious
did my spokes trickle about an autumnal blast
obdurately garrisoning what was meant to be
an entirely different season.
The place seemed empty
as if Nobody lived there, ever.
This occasionally became the problem
that most obsessed me yet deterred not my sprees
for the purposes we choose
are constantly abandoned by flocculent mischance
as the weather—like a jawbone
being pressed felly into slick mud—compounds our sense of definition
that hums around unavailable parents.
The action continues bereft of cause; the face
of shamed hewers melt.
But if in a fairer spell reclaim you I could, then I
in a January would.

Winter

Don't give up your shibboleth:
we are united in our strangeness
to each other;
walking miles apart, just
to be together, accidentally, together.
You have to believe in difference
and that, except in odd moments
of grace,
we are fine threads, separately
woven into a pattern
that we will never understand.

Modernism

We simultaneously realized that your armpits smelled like semen
—and? That's as far as the story goes.
Phatic marshaling surpassed my expectations with regards to
how my mark is carved in the trunk of expensive harm.
Edenic references that only existed in my solipsistic woolgathering
were transposed to the realm of experience in the capacity
of an amateur comedian bombing before a crowd of debutantes.
You held a lorgnette against my hirsute chest and smirked
again, at the amusement park, again until your gender politics
strung inverted like a rabbit in the window of some butcher shop.
You hissed at me your premiere insult: "You fucking *modernist*!"
Queerly relieved that everyone who knew me in the world
had reached the same conception of my self that I curtained
(ruinous, discomfiting, emptily defensive, in love with my weaknesses)
I jumped off the top of the gothic cathedral of my loneliness
and landed below in a hundred pieces on the tongue
jutted from a dick-sucking maw of satanic absorption.
All of this is to say that you cut my hair
in the 10th arrondissement, the home of a retired ophthalmologist
and the last time I said I loved you I meant it as a spiteful riposte.
What other memories do I have of the nights before the nights?
—only that your brother spent years weeping into my maquillage
before I told him solemnly he had to go home.

Brooklyn

If you want to ruin me, Brooklyn, do so with love
waiting for a public language in my small yellow room
a confident bus ruling down strafed avenues
upon which an unwholesome fog has alighted
pictures and the bleats of anxious children in puffy jackets
frowning women walking through the black smoke
confirming an underground electrical fire.

Gallons of two percent milk mixed with Ballantine Ale
the adamantine smell of calamitous blood
rushing skyward from the gutters through the floor
rats, millions of them, and forgiveness.

You give me shelter and fugitive boys, their skin
the transient laurels with which I carpet my tongue
you give me the forsaken technology I use to constitute
and cry out frivolities back into the wheat of your hair
your shape stupendous is that of indefatigable shticks
psychotic as it is friendly, forecastable as it is profound
the walls of an empty cinema could collapse into the street
spraying dust and debris into the faces of the gentry
and the food stamp recipients, the nomadic hipsters
slinking about, ashing cigarettes into the decayed brush
limping from pavement cracks in front of monstrous hospitals
but everything would be bright yet, I'd puke patchouli and blood
on the entrance for another evangelical bookstore.

Relay your provincial promise like a sting behind my sinuses
ravage me with bright fulfillment, when I nest in your sweaty arms
grasp my throat and tell me this is how you leave me alone
you make me feel like a picked zit that just won the Nobel Prize
I know what I trust, I know what it is I'm doing here
a half-dead cat swallows a stone and runs into traffic
the car swerves and the driver thinks about his next appointment.

You appreciate atrabilious wounds and represent beauty
the bitten-raw cuticles of a sure man caressing his own future
and the paving stones fatted on cheap handles of wine
that howl drunk depths into his loopy ears
just another crazy person quietly trying to choose life
because what else is there to do, where the sky is green
but to know this, that my skeleton will melt jokingly
into your ambitious will and, as we all do around these parts
come to rest on the cushion of a negligent day
I say your name sixteen times when I pray.

Power

Awake in your draped and sunless room. The rando
from last night tugs his boxers up his legs, pulls thinly
on a one-hitter, asks, "Why isn't the electricity working?"
The difference between the glorious illumination past
midnight and the pathetic resignation of the stripped morn
is the number of miles between your neighborhood and
the Con Edison garage where they park their evil trucks.
Unable to keep the lights on, you joke, "I'm running out
of things to go wrong!" Then your gums start bleeding
then you get fired, rent bounces, you blackout again
and lose your phone. Then another friend dies, this
time in California: an excitable poet you ran into last
on Valencia, in the Mission; she threw her arms apart
and screamed, "You're going to win the Pulitzer Prize!"
Her stomach so inhabited by tumors she looked pregnant.
Again, find yourself with nothing to show for it but
a series of stolen umbrellas from work (and a few
impending court dates). Man, this city hates poets!
Walking up to the bodega counter with a comically large
bottle of cheap beer, throw your last three bucks down
next to the gruff couple haggling over the price of a
single condom. Stalk back to your desperate garret
under the discretion of a cold February moon, obscene
and maximized, bullied on either side by slim parentheses
of cloud. It's okay to like the dark, but don't let it keep you.

The Blot

Dear chowderhead, O darling limp-wristed Termagant
culminate under the jilted pergolas of a deep schlep
this is my hammer for forgiving, this for giving up.
Foul tournaments swim around the extent of white poverty
put a gun in the hand of a child and send him over that high fence
daunted and mewling like some backwards soliloquy
guzzling down creosol and thick syrup from your tree
another night of vaudevillian trespass, another ashtray
slipped into the coat check girl's blouse like a tip.
I don't want to hear anything unless it is about that
I don't want to speak unless my subject is destructive and obtuse.
Small chairs! The chairs are too fucking small, I tell you!
Who designed these chairs? was he one foot tall?
O, here comes the armed kid back from the wasteland
blood drooling down his now manic face, but he's out of ammo
he did something out there that we'll never comprehend
because there is no language for this kind of savagery
as it is concurrently subtle and blunt, then it disappears for a while
then it comes back, behind the eyes or hidden under a tiny chair.
Dear mongrel, my dissolute arms wrapped round your bosom
another frame cradled in your unsightly winch—carry me away
from this place, like a snoozing baby out of the gates of Disneyland
it's over, it's over, and yet it has hardly begun. The blot!

True Love

How in over your head do you have to be
to contact the fur, and how far back do you have to go
to engender the blue facility in a former eye?
The pedestal'd inamorato won't ever grovel and will
only flit through the surfaces of coeval fastenings
whirred speculations concerning not an ideal but a fulcrum
finally whispers haunting the corner of the mien
of whoever you happen to meddle with, skunk.
The arc of a piss has given up more secrets
and as for clarity of style or purpose, count it baldly out
this is the dirty life, the answer under the integument
the kind of thing you learn to let be embarrassing, ignored
the reason why babies are deposited in dumpsters
and untethered reprobates left out to dry.
How do we exculpate ourselves in a litigious world
that gnaws away the palate and the bone, leaves dust
—how do we manipulate such post-industrial smut
into the shape of something that we can live with?
Listen, I want you, whoever you are, be you found
in a singular form or cast across a graphed sea of glimpses
you are the basal part of me I forswore for some membership
but if I can strain ten thousand heavens, if only in theory
I have to hold you, I have to bleed into you and say
I love you the way fire makes light.

Back to the Future

A curious teenage coincidence
who's fixing to make this town sorry
maybe the urge for revenge
ruined us so completely
we forgot the original crime
tell me what you want to hear
but I cannot stop on a dime
sure our parents fucked us up
our leaders are wanton and wild
better to be an angry adult
than a cold, complacent child

Droll behemoths in the landscape
lunching on the lethal form of
the drowsy incumbency; *peace!*
be with they who take the seed
and place a curse upon the flower

Your saliency has become franchised
looked in those eyes and was surprised
never trust banks inside hospitals
dreaming of fortunate days
rock star horizons and infinite moms
are part of this game that we play

Joy

I might as well admit that I want it this way
it shouldn't have worked out with us
he who buys a house begins to fear what's outside of it
cause and effect will effloresce inside unknown weapons
mud and complicity
the triumph of living just another day, think about that
to stand before Moloch, declaring yourself a poet...
        Put your hands behind your head and rise slowly
(well, this is going to hurt).
But it's not just a minor universe making love to itself
different people recognize the fulvous plains differently
accommodation doesn't tell us that we see it
the time of day may escape my mouth inopportunely
bodies are sure to amuse before they have to leave
what we have right now is all that we're going to get
the trick isn't figuring out, it's falling in love
        The blindest joy is pregnant with stirring design
to cherish and burst away.

Prospect Park After Dark

u sing; here in the felonious brush, dither and spew (speculate
turn, tame like a caged animal with a little blood on her fang)
aureate rings hang like hair out of the varmint of suburbia
they say who gives a fuck, it's all done online these days
sling quietly through the wilderness, become different services
pretend u are not alone walking through a tenebrous vault
there are going to be some lights until the lights go out
even when there isn't money—sex and hunger, they remain
remember the spring we all got lost in the park after dark
we loved each other's purple teeth and lack of driver's permits
it was like the trees held us through our ages, like they donated
the future into the wrinkled mouth of a muggy knoll, doubt that
then one of us got shot in the head, another drowned, go figure
all's here for u—at least in theory or over the phone but the
tears going on, they're harder than the GRE they sting they
turn buff or reddish in the holler of our pristine feminism
walk on the grass, swim into the lip of the polluted lake
climb branches, kiss, break up, break down, download
fall asleep in the passenger seat, lord knows where we are
experience, they say, is passé—how many bridges have damaged
poor thunder and denied the blood and tiny creatures that lurk
under the skin, in the creases of our eyelids, in our stool
u cannot imagine what's in the woods or facsimile of aforesaid
it's the cost, calling from a jail cell in California, turning around
and telling the kids it's only fathom it's only the end of the world
oh u reservoir, how that fatigues and how it charms, discovery
passes us, the forestry survives the night, the critters writhe
u are going to have to walk into campaign and take sides.

On the Beauty and Terror of Images

Spirit of the damn golden world
symmetries' celestial promises
faith without works is nothing
when all you have
is your grip
on the knife
and you feel the need to wake up or else
there's a reptile urge to pulverize
evidences of inharmonious grift
frustrations and misconduct
stitched into the tapestry of involvement
an aesthetic calculus too hermetic
for the need of a quorum
ratios pulse through our political voracity
I'm the child of a killer
reaching into an abstract sky
and withdrawing a ructious cup
full of tepid liquid sourced
from the stream of friendship
as passive figures are impaled
on the reaching spikes of creatures' arms
like syringes full of drain cleaner
everything we trusted demolished and gone
the sky as red as the blood on your hands
not forgiven.

Hooded Man

The peace that passes understanding gets hollowly exploded, sound
I feel nothing as I walk through the garden or outside of its gates
doubt the walls, live on the moon, tell interest and say the names
I'm not too young to kill people, kill myself, live in a country
that is half of what it says it is and otherwise the death of recognition
we go about our daily passes and degenerate, guys die all the time
children, lovers, other humans—echo somehow always castrating
presence and the epicenter of disaster where you don't really know
what's going to give or going on or the media crush that brays sent
shadows, however the earth still moves, and we plant our sums
we hook our believed fingers into the mouth of sake to chew the nail
it's funny, living in the gutter and dreaming of joy—the world escapes
into humor and eventuality, streak, dare yourself to become its face
I went to school too, accrued my debt, a plane flew over me
it sent a bomb on a drive into pregnant frenzy, friends did not help it
divide and the restoration, our forefathers never passed around, crap
I don't care if people care about my life I just want to die for a reason
grow up, trouble out the tribes, let sand and loam fill your lungs
listen, legs will go flying, then they will go still, the streets of the land
drink the blood of the fallen, and it's okay because we are waiting
but it's not okay because we don't know what we're waiting for
if you see a man you hate put a hood on him and don't ask questions.

Mystery Novels

The killer left us a clue in the metadata
the entire malice of a drained contention
like children having to take binocular risks
in the sullen classroom, a deft preparation
for the intractable dissension of elements
we're reassuring the masculine interests
all this violence, crowds screaming at once
paying for unsustainable so-called solutions
given into the dynamic hatred and the flame
that covers a pre-teen brain, god went insane
the night the Lindbergh baby disappeared
we live in fear, so what, so take my hand and
retire into obedience, unless anyone loves
unless you can organize grief and misconduct
deal with sociopathic management, bad genre
decisions flare the evasive breath of my loss
the head honchos miscalculated the cost
Los Angeles reduced to rubble in the process
I don't know, kids, I feel like a giant mess
maybe I should go home, wait it's destroyed
the oceans started to boil, all the fish died
of herpes, radioactive superstorms ravaged
the land, the faithful went mad and shredded
their enemies, and what did I even do today?
drank, fucked, wept, thought about Euripides
and wandered into a meadow of absolute crime
where cherubs kissed my thighs and told me
"Welcome Home."

Remembering

My dad always treats me like shit—so what
His mother lost her memory, strapped to a chair
The entire lineage wailed through history
Like spoilt white babies pissing themselves
All calling out the same marbled passage:
"Teach me how to overcome evil passions
And become a saint!" I remember a time when
What was said mattered and it mattered how
You said it and why, but now that I think of it
Nobody actually told me that, it was just
An assumption, a way of getting around.

The reality is that we are all spinning wildly into the void.

My friends save my life but can only do so much
Most of me remembers parts of you—it hurts but
Love is more than obligation, and wounds of
Removal shall be assuaged in the vagueness
Inherent in the bodies of others, everything changes
What was safe becomes dangerous, the wolf of
Youth claws into the fabric of basic survival.
These memories are our way of understanding
What will never return, cheap and haunting
Yet don't look for me rehearsing what I would say
Were I to meet you again on the street in the rain.

Following Spring

après Rimbaud

After the conceptual flood expired
suspects slank in the shifting remnants
and puked a prayer at the rainbow'd air
through the valley of the nest of spiders.
Hey, hilarious prizes
hidden in the peeping weeds
near the seminal juncture
where slayers rose
who pulled their vessels down
to the biblical sea, like flickers shown.
Blood consuming, veins a home
for antiretrovirals, butt pirates
or fucking circuses
where the big guy upstairs
fogs windshields with stinky breathing.
Ichor all over, as lactose leaked
creatures constructed. Morning
coffee in a cardboard cup
billowing in our clutches, we
smoked before shuttered storefronts
like severe children enthralled by memes.
A door slammed shut in Union Square
baby wants attention, clinched
as weather under the broken tower
bathing in sparkling rills of pee.
When you find a stranger in the Alps
the swollen church communicates
a bunch of smiling tablatures.

Hordes escaped the splendid hostels
we made in night's frozen misrule.
Again, the moon harked
species warning through time's desert
don't cry for me, Argentina
bemoaned the estate.
Then the violent forest
begrudgingly told me it was spring.
Unhearing lagoon surges
losing bridges, unloosing roots
like a dark blanket
absorbing corpses
gay bash the mountain
wet misery climbs to meet its flood.
Since we broke up
cosmetics of us
juicily unfurled.
It's... boring
and the Wicked Witch of the West
who lights us up
won't let us in on the secret
or tell us otherwise.

Street of Flowers

Once again she has to insist that it's not your fault
proffering a sigh that tells you exactly what you need
to know about the color of the argument, the timbre
of the times. Perfect, getting stoned in the salon
just passing fancy in an unused salle a manger
slipping my hand beneath your collar in the atelier
listening to new records in the older sister's chambre
getting too intimate with the raggedy furniture.
She might as well catch a glimpse of you before
there's nothing left to see, not that any of us have
ever lost faith in your ability for production
it's just that the grass is so overgrown you get
lost in the front yard, you wake up several times
a day. She is in the upper room, brushing her teeth
getting rid of the fractious smack of last afternoon
wilting like that plant in the corner we never water
but still in love—or, at least, still capable of being in it.
I don't hold it against you for taking my face in your hands
we don't have to figure out the relationship; we have
to accept that this is an absolutely landlocked county
and, as per local ordinance, no structure shall be built
higher than our memorial obelisk in the insalubrious park
now: everybody who lives here knows what they did
the dead, well, they have their own jobs to perform.
You obey her siren call down the boulevard, floating
behind it like Bugs Bunny after a whiff of rhubarb pie
we're all sweethearts now, the pockets gross with cash

there are things we let go and, gracile, things we catch
I haven't put much thought into it since the accident
you haven't touched her clavicle since prom night
and that was so long ago you forget what it tastes like.

Treatment

After a while the way the pills rattled
in their bottle started to get to him
each morning a grating jingle
at the medicine cabinet
he came to hate that noise and all it represents
the doctor did not seem surprised
when the results came back
and he confessed a lapse
and the reason why
leaving not to return
she had been treating men since the beginning
and, frankly, seen it all before.

So that's how *he* died, the other guy
was afraid to get tested
so he never did
and when his friends saw lesions on his neck
they thought, "No, it couldn't be..."
he got defensive at the suggestion
he go to the doctor
he didn't have a doctor
even after the first time he collapsed
and Stephanie drove him to the hospital
at his funeral everybody was like
"How did this happen?"

Cost of Living

It makes me tired to purchase
And I'm traumatized by money
Always spending something
Never getting the math right
I tread Chinatown in spring
Let busyness surge o'er my body
Conduct business with the weather
If I could trade a million Januaries for now
Code switching within my own inner monologue
I would stalk up the dark and kiss you
Fuck the lights out of you, turn your electricity off
My anger is a delicious affliction
Command this vessel, I am responsive
Can we afford the prognosis and
What gets put back on the shelf?
        [The next sound is indescribable]
Surprised that I had any currency left
I walked into the great hall of life with a confident gait
Nobody wants to live in the fire
It's one of the things that is done to survive.

Mother's Day

The treacherous sting of
the ungratified memory
purging humility from a breath
stops meaning
or at least fades it out
into the last bulwark of a song
we barely recognize
there was some instinctual function
an animality betrayed
in the complication of taction
and the way our orderless emotions
snarled wetly across the bow
of knowing each other.

I ignored you
forsook your love
and used you up
smiling.

Parents don't have to kill
themselves to raise a child
children never learn
not to destroy
what came before
not in this country.

I had to build a wall
around the pain
but walls don't work
the very concept of a wall
is insane.

Russian Boys on the Q Train

You are a stupid coward and your heart is full of bullshit and mud
how many years is it going to take for me to write what I wanna write
bless me and bless the kids these days, they stray, they turn it out
if you want to know why I live here then you have to listen to music
multifarious asking doesn't put a brain into the largesse or the voice
I only choose to be stuck on the Q train with two Russian boys
poking and screaming at each other, stepping out of their tennis shoes
waltzing to the puzzled tune of the Manhattan Bridge, Bronx-bound
I walk with you daily but I have no idea where any of us are going
I don't know if you belong in one of those porn videos or selling
my own breaths back to me in a caisson full of worldly resentment.

The Machine

A demon of summer, laced child
with hayfield loops of hair
beholding her father's razor
in the opposite of the sun
praying diligently for an arrival
of our vast nemesis
there are biological, psychological
and social factors
to the matter
but the militarized weight
of corporate recourse
smashes everything as flat, as smooth
as the face of a porcelain doll
you try to live here
balancing work, family, and pleasure
while the merciless roaming eye
floats over the waters
shooting lasers into traffic
in a state of perpetual war
it's nuts—we feed our blood
into the machine
and watch it boil
and come out clean
as if this weren't the end to begin with.

Bowery Hero

Poet, without bed or house
Ruminates on ex-boyfriends
And drinks bottles of Ballantine
At the edge of a friend's loft
Here above the Bowery, watches
Commerce truly scrape the life
Out of the screaming recesses
Veined among hulked property
Plastic, paralyzed, from a pocket
Brined in privilege and alcohol
Pretenders and sluts rushing loss
Like light passing through objects
Declares a religion in the mouth
Tight corners deliberate with flesh
A few attempting to do it right
The rest surrendered to doubt
Manhattan unhand this sanity
Preserved as a ruby in velvet
Saviors of ambiguous intention
Must pace the ginormous span
To prove that the ability exists
To at least begin covering ground
An altered sense of night rising
Out of a hole in liberty's face
The bridge is a drunken tongue
Taking him in hot discordance
Luckless generation frightens
As concrete gets lost in itself.

Summery

Gross guarded goblins are gobbling my goals
There's naught but madness and slick liability
In the ears of the urchins of the terrible littoral
Somehow scooped out and drowned by shoals

You have to accept it, cloaked in tangent mist
Grease and bad manners trailing after a wish
That lobs and robs and ricochets contaminant
Parsing divisible corners to oppositional slant

Smash a slice of insecure climate softly divined
Into the leader's scorched marketable brain
Don't dare regret the lost seasons of touch
We both know that everything costs too much

Eternal circumvention washed off in the rain
All those newer to the dislocating protocol
Reported to me that he is holding a weapon
Soaking it up, writing out his confession

Return to Fire Island

The ocean is as cold as she could be and bitchily recondite
now come back here to this blue world
crawling with concupiscent boys
and brave men and the elders, mangy deer posing in the sward
things used to be easier, some kinds of sex came handier
high tea was higher
I've forgotten everything—dislocated in the Sunken Forest
enjoy running up the Grove, chased through the Meat Rack by a fox
watching Frank on the dunes, in them, under the tires
swooning into a guest bedroom
a vial of poppers leaking
into the red wine stain
on the white carpeted floor
another life to receive, another beach to sow
yet another underwear party
I have seen the strains of a boy's cum floating in a champagne flute
and have walked the calcined shore to Lonelyville and points south
if it's like this at summer's end
ascend and grovel
and wait the winter out
queer swans spitting on the docks of the Pines
a townie kid prowling for a drink on the deck
sometimes I said I knew who trafficked in glory
or the moon looked like it would dive into the sea
there is a burden to this fantasy but it's one we want to weather
I am a prince, I can take it, I can wreck him in the shower
shoving it all in
to tan under the boiling welkin
reading a book about what the Greeks did
knowing what the waves are for

experience suspended and slatted aboveground
who owns this pleasure and how much does it cost
who wants to share
the tears and glory that bring me here
to no end
to be subsumed by our nature
and finally flung herky-jerky into the Atlantic
to join our dying fathers.

Breezy Point

Storm waters drowned the beachside 9/11 memorial
and retired cops' vacation homes burned down
in what felt like a metaphor for our relationship
but was a lurid squall blasting against the dirty shores.
I watched security footage of power lines sparking
flailing into the surge as flame licked helpless roofs
basements flooded with ocean and sewage
yet still we felt safe holding each other in bed
as the whole building swayed gently in the wind.
I have loved you on beaches that no longer exist
we left a rental van in somebody's driveway
jumped a fence for private access to the sea
smoked a joint as neighbors eyed us suspiciously
buried our toes in the sand and listened to the waves
but fragile things like that are liable to change.
The weather is perfect about four weeks a year
and buildings rise like glass stalks downtown
as we grow older and away from each other
this feels like we're rehearsing for the big one
it's not true that nobody knew what we were in for.

Peter Does Not Listen

Clean clothes, Peter punch a cop, you do not listen
capitulating to Marfa, you touch the side of my hair
and the government, darling die young, this place has
so few uses for you, Peter the way you dance in that
dress, it takes four bottles of Ballantine to write a poem
it takes a wolf to stalk the hollow bones of physical
sciences, the last time Peter was on time immoderate
twirls set themselves around the regal cast, an organ
and another organ—just kind of communing, full blooded
and unsophisticated, like twelve out of body experiences
and a metastasized diamond, like always, like dark fantasy
like little Peter sitting on a saturated log, how did they
keep warm (our ancestors), how did they conceive of
themselves, maybe it bothered them maybe it did not
maybe they crushed through the candy store, bit a swan
made fun of the humidity in your precipitate denouncement
precious avifauna don't need this in their life, something
lasts (but what), something turns into the horse apples and
Chickasaw kickshaws that our daddies bulldozed with great
aplomb during the unspeakable administration, Peter play
in the culverts, covered in shit, you would do anything to
get yourself out of this tight spot, but baby you're about to
give me a heart attack with every lick around the corner of
my ear, and maybe we want it that way—replete with pomp
the fetor of deteriorating preoccupations, and all his regret.

Nonsense

Take your refuge in language—throw yourself off a bridge
meridians and digital succotash straw out inviolate biology
not what money means to the planet but what it means to me
who is going to fight for the criterion in gloaming inauguration
it's hard when you are producing everything but what you need
abrogated sedition like drinking a pop on a regional jet to die
ere long lonelinesses spin prevailing listeners toward expiration
nobody names but the namer and our cells divide unevenly
the witness never told the jury the scope of what he knew
it won't be possible to understand what's happening until much later.

Hung Up on You

It takes a little light or a kiss by the fountain near Defender's Arch
some red spiders playing in the grass or across a granite sundial
stints and hoary motes
to draw away romantic impressions of past lives.
I guess half a year isn't such a long time
kids and their majestic vices
take over the hostile campus, arrive un-punctually
fulfill messed-up prophecies
acting out an ancient comedy dressed in juice-stained robes
and lampooning their devilry, selfsame as mine: stinging, ascendant.
How bad did my habits bother you
how oft do I dash through your mind?
I'm left loitering on Gertrude Stein's grave
like a day at the beach, kind but lugubrious
fake tears parading down a slope through Pere Lachaise
and it takes a little getting away and coming back again to rediscover
the locker wherein I squirreled all of my private shit and confidence
like the sick remains of an infant queen kept disguised in a shale vault
the flesh turns to dirt
the dirt begets the dandelions
but cudgel thy brains no more about it
for your dull ass will not mend his pace with beating.
South Brooklyn is a burning cake in summer, my arms are empty
my jealousies chandelier into recurrent damage
well, it's got to be that way.
Don't be too forgiving of strangers but don't give up on love
don't fall asleep on the subway
don't forget your umbrella, that's a storm cloud
that's the ghost of the fire, that's not anything we could readily ignore
like the visions, at which point it doesn't quite matter

if you went back to her or were slain by goons on the outskirts of town:
in my bed, under the Williamsburg Bridge, on the meadow
where Whitman once spilled his seed
and Crane co-mingled with a sailor
            I found you there.

Ex-Boyfriend on the Beach

I pissed on a church the blameless ships and the bough
twisted away; I kissed you in the narthex for sandy
seconds, cruised into the ocher culpability of summary
tributes *there is a lingering government in this* fade
out for pixels may sting they may wake you nightly
"trust" blisters, dematerializes, the magic of your brain
roasting under a long prospect of crystal stars, as if
a dawn was made for us or surrendering, fettered gulls
given into the sea, the sweat on a can of diet soda
that sort of thing, your coarse tongue enjoying the ridges
of the roof of my mouth and the hustle the ride it takes
producers, poetasters, and the emergence of a new
vernacular, what the all-seeing eye cannot capture
the fictional source crowding my view from this
time share *pull the strings* your sunglasses dip
down the bridge of your nose, sweat mixed with
sunscreen and semen splashes into your eye
and from a nostalgic and forlorn vantage I watch
the endless slideshow, ersatz vacations, pictures of
you turning somersaults, becoming gold in the bonny
glow of another *yet another* fucking impossible beach
the fantasy of a finch with a potato chip in her mouth
the day that I know I need to meet you at the end of

The Road to the Temple of Honour and Fame

Does a diamond desire itself?
The eagle that we thought we knew
escaped in a frigate, preparing to live
vibrancy and rise, just to say and try it out.
While we might as well, might not
it does not seem that you learned from your own example
men and woman and a stroll through the morass
small counties, piteous churches, lurching
you're not going to be able to stand up to this.
What is the thing that we need, what is it
is it what I take from you when I touch your cheek
or what disappears before me in the dank cave?
Put your hand inside me and become political
caress a hapless farmhand in the outhouse
at the edge of the formal property, attain
or arrive on the bus every day like the rest of them
we all come on the bus we all bow down to masters
of how we do, how we work it out, windows.
I don't know about you but I was born
to burn the land up
chock full of sin and wonderment
and right now all I want to do is walk along the street
with you and cogitate my small rebellions
I was alone until I met this guy on the Down Low
asked his HIV status, he said, "I don't know none of that shit."
His grandma was in the living room, he cried
as he fucked me, I used it as cruel fuel, I dreamt
that my mother took me to the cinema to see Snow White
when I was a little child, buckled up in the back seat
bellowing for alternative monies and preparation

savage as it is, it is the stand, it is where it is going
desire, desire, desire, give me the Supreme Court
give my dad a simpler time when men were men
and a boy could fend off comestible hegemony
by one wave of his magic wand in the parking lot
the eagle opens and clutches, we make the relationship.
We go away, let a formidability pass and spread
put you on the floor girl you are good, you're dead.
I will make a hundred mistakes and fuck grace
before it is gone away, before it is generated and mad.
We are your unqualified guardians, motion for the speaker
on the previous question to table the appeal
on the outstanding parliamentary procedure
to foreclose the following vote for
the approaching amendment for procedure
forecloses and proceeds to the ground
and gets made to be a worse species of your unconscious love.

Men in Bed

A room full of middling friends looking out for each other
Work of a flat earth and easiness, used to transgress
In the swimming relief of tautological arguments
Perverts invaded every facet and reports proved the worst
Yet you took off your shirt to mitigate aquiline heralds
Youth draped over the body like a borrowed fur coat
There remains the refrain of boys but laughter doesn't last
They compare flawless surfaces and dig in wet mouths
Fruited by the value neutrality of the middle of the night
Garb those who mortgage in the waste of disputation
Monetized scuffling upsets the bowels of corporate mania
Dismantled by a child who foresees in the inky well
A time when you will come to want for men in bed.

Good Dog

Bully the defenses, the chains I forge in life
decorating my throat and clenching tight
fixation, malice, resentment rips asunder
good intentions, y'know most of 'em are out
for themselves. Appreciate what led you here
temporarily stunned by the peripheral glories
breezed past in the demand for progression
and growth; aren't we all disappointed by the
unconscious strictures of this environment?
It's getting harder to believe in anything
when everything's unstable and vagarious
as apparently the factory setting for humanity
is genocidal destruction—a particularity of
our species, getting rid of a problem by proxy
trying to beat our hatred of ourselves out of
someone else's face. This kind of dance is
performed only by lovers in the moonlight
menacing the climate with inexplicit doom
no use comparing present conditions with
the expectations you developed based upon
previous reports of similar experiences.
Wake me up when rubber meets steel, I'll
protect the meal, retral potentialities, seas
bleached out and cancerous, full o' needles
pantomiming safety at the cusp of bad play
fugitive force tracing itself up the lines of
vulnerary dispatch. I admired the sultry
approach of the calculated horde, broached
scars for stars for irrational presentiment
a fan club made up of your worst enemies.

Innocence

some rep with the total bard
if this guy won't love me then I'm against gay marriage
leave me like this
my pancake makeup dripping down my visage like a melting witch
life peeps and shakes her fires in the burdened air:
shillelagh the impulses and
bludgeon me bro, I'm used to it, it gives me a semi
it makes me take toys out
so tired of refulgence so bored of taking pills
the plane ride to Paris
makes me nostalgic
the busy presumer has no time for sorrow
the kid is bleeding out of a hole in his forehead
not sure we believe that much in the ancient poets anymore
nor the voice of reason
there are simply always going to be giants in the dirty chamber
merging the message
draw my redemption in lipstick across a twink's face
shoot him again with a gun
can't keep this up, careening precipitously and unwilling
into adulthood, ready to die
kiss my ass after upholstering my rectum with crystals
you can still live this down
let it change you—*l'amour toujours*—wait, no, go fuck yourself
roll away on a bike
as easy as Satan's temper all the night suppressed
and let it be so heard on earth
I will always love you but I will never accept you
also can you validate my parking
everything is vulgar and stuffed like a sour clam full of iniquity

obviate it, remember
when I was but an eager lad
I let place feed me its joy but now am too famous and
that's an acquainted plage, deliquesced and seen
that is a horse of a different color!

Bending Over Backward

Who says it has to be low or work from the consequence back
to a sugary capstan of winter light mowing over Bow Bridge
cracking a wide seam down the thin mean of our privileged youth
those symphonies of easy felicity, such jealously remembered but
un-regained luck? This is not the story of how we simply ruined it
but of out of tune instruments bending over backward to say
something is the matter and we love it and we're going away.
Remember how founded a rock felt when I felt his skin on it
and the easy terror of moss settling on a plate, lives like cormorants
who says we had lives like diving bells, rendered as vague and
ducky as a tossed-off picnic some Sunday when the sun fit in our
pants and postmodernity seethed around us like a rib-tickling gadget
divorced from praxis and prominence, when the concept won?
Sensation, small breaths into each other's mouths, pleasure and
transgression—everything spelled out in front of the golden minor
as simple and lowering as an unreciprocated hug from a dead lover.
Who says that is our creditor when the arms of the ageless oaks
sway still and the possibility of new silviculture abounds each
time the beautiful room collapses into the future like an arch wave.
The violin was once a fearsome spruce and she will be again.

Play Is Labor

Seeking damages
or an injunction
to cease and desist
this harassment
you think you'll be
cured but you won't
the meaning of wellness
will simply redefine
over time around you
many food service workers
in this city are homeless
most of the gays
at this club
are busted up
and half have daddy issues
unremarkable in their pleasure
and hardly remembered
it gets to the point
where the only way
to get anyone's attention
is by hurting them
which does not
leave us well-served
the truth is that this is work
because play is labor
and labor is joy.

The Emperor, He Had Total Control

Within me I harbor a deep unforgivable empathy for Jeffrey Dahmer
a cognizance of how such stilted alienation could so wickedly labor
when a wound drinks itself into homicidal solipsism
and builds a throne out of utopian skulls
in a downmarket Wisconsin living room.
I know the blood of the life of the jilted mind
I know how to make the misery a kingdom
this dark magic, this negative power
is forged in lonely ambles through the catacombs of propriety
influence unearned but achieved by toxic hazing
grueling privilege scalds to ash the verdant countryside.
A rented room, a sick alley, brunette corners of an unwholesome club:
there I am, with you, drilling a tiny hole into your brain
trying to make you into something
I can finally control, a zombie, the only being I believe I can love.
Come back to my place with me for beer and company
gore like chocolate
hot sperm crying down the brown nudity of a corpse
unhouseled, lessening.
Skin dissolves in acid
bones by a sledgehammer are crushed into powder
what I can take as the evidence of my capacity
I will enshrine with laurels or gaudy spray paint
but the proof of my hunger and my failure must be
disposed of in simmering barrels
tucked underground, inside recesses
flushed down the toilet, the hair sealed in bags
each lip eaten—penises separated.
A rabid beast stalks down the main avenue of this pathetic town
and citizens cower in buses

and behind the smudged glass of public foyers.
No disaster is as complete
as the gorgeousness of my imagined dominion
I will destroy in my small reality
what you could never possibly begin to fashion
and in doing so in my kitchen, through evil experiments
I have made this part of my fascination
something to be reckoned with
and in sharing it with you
we're alive, famous, full of light.
We kill what we can in our own way, we live and kill what we can
(because otherwise there's never any chance).
I yearn, and I want to be touched, and to love
but worlds won't have me
when the lightening shoots out of the emperor's hands
remember
—it's only a movie.

Falling

We only made of ourselves what we could understand
being young hurts and then you don't know what to do
about what gets expected of you and your whole contract
with society, the way the trash disappears every Wednesday
and we pay the salaries of scared men with loaded guns
the governments of the globe are awake and hungry
I spent a summer subsisting off food stamps, baloney
and bread—blowjobs and booze are cheaper than
whatever you're trying to offer, necessary stranger
and then I woke up to realize that he'd walked away
maybe I'm not a writer anymore, maybe I am falling
down a perpetual staircase, jumping off a bridge
to nowhere, making decisions that are just okay enough
to keep me merely alive, trying not to hurt anyone around
me too seriously as we rapidly deteriorate, no it's fate
yet the moon—so exhausting to write about!
without context there's no getting back, no way
free of this obligation to keep it up sans direction
or support, because everyone who cared about you is dead
and your friends are collapsing in waves of otherness
once I sought out the sensation of a desperate kiss
and my lips have touched those of men from everywhere
their various fingers always pulling through my hair
nothing compares to having my body taken seriously
and I haven't found any better communion than this
or path away from the gentle miseries my kind endures.

Hipster Slave Boy

Could it have been the lady in the red hat
who slunk phlegmatic out of the room
meaning to latterly caress the childhoods
of so many disabused apparatchiks
with her rose-colored and slightly spattered glove
who stood within the domaine
and clucked and peddled the air with sniveling reproof
and squandered a box full of animal skulls?—No
twas not her but her contumacious sister. Never forget.
Love stays, we together lie on an unsatisfactory air mattress
backs against exposed brick
watching a video wherein two appealing dudes
maneuver out of their shorts
and flop down on a soft bed, rubbing the luscious towers
that've grown out of their crotches
presently folding into each other and gyrating
beefing out phrases in
splintered American English
("Oh yah bay-bay, thas roit, fuch mey, fuch mey!").
That's basically what sex is, that is what I think it is
that's how I make sense of it.
Could it have been a thread of your shore-tinted hair
wrapped around a tree like a cheap rental car
on a holiday weekend two miles outside of a college town
that bestirred my loins and racked my inclination
sent me on a woebegone five day cruise
some midwestern ninny won
by being the hundredth caller on a daytime radio show
that buildings bobbed down for
that was the true cause of this here war

in which the kingdom has been entrenched for countless generations?
Yes.
Yes, by god, and then some.
I can never remember the face I'm supposed to have
when I wake up alone of mornings
but I'm jaundiced and dancing in the shadows.
You wouldn't know what to do with me, bub
if you ever decoded my taradiddles
I wouldn't trade this feeling for all the champagne
inside the Brooklyn Bridge.

The Last Poem

The last poem I read addressed the yearning of skin
in a fine-spun, tender series of lacquered metaphors
that splashed pastel blotches across my flaxen sight
I looked the other way and a developer swooped in
prideful of his theft and scorning the injured margin
chemicals we pump into our blood won't prevent it
from developing into an outrageous demonstration
of the way reality cracks open and dissolves before
the fearsome and absurd brutality of late capitalism
compressed into the wriggly mess of an uptown train
on the morning commute, eyes bouncing, the lights
whipping past in the dingy tunnel, I start heaving
the poem printed on a poster vibrating behind me
mocks the singular boredom of our daily existence
with pastoral mentions of clean streets and careful
citizens organizing for a collective benefit, sloping
over the bogus details, and listening to grievances
justly tendered, hope for a provisional instrument
to stave off the reckoning but the bill remains due
sentimentalism suggests that despite a general feeling
we are in it together, and nothing's tedious, say I still
wouldn't love you if you were the last poem on earth.

Honey in a Zoo

Berserk but suspended in aspic, the animals are on fire & parading
up and down the thoroughfare that terminates at a celebratory arch
& all monuments finally bleed together, confuting what was only
to begin with a shriveled contribution—the earth loves it like plastic
asphodels, like pyrite, like honey in a zoo. The floppy disk contains
all the plenipotentiary's secrets & is buried under the magnolia trees
at the dead man's end of the fen, where the swan hisses disappointed
at her babies, wishing they'd grow up to fly into the Chrysler Building
or anything worth bragging about in the annual Christmas newsletter.
Arcadian as the middle manager who wears mismatched stockings
& smells of piss slathered with dime store astringent, asking after
the determinant—however realizing one can take it from one source
& from a series of other, oppositional, sources, till the big picture pans
out as discrepant, swarming, & awesome as an abstract expression
(it needs some polish but there's nobody for the job right now, as the
journeymen, lion tamers, & philosophers are occupied in the bread line)
sic the crisis is rested in this. Better abscond with the bodies of the local
virgins before the dust settles—Noah is reviewing the quarterly losses
wishing now he'd kept his big mouth shut; all living things, sounding;
The cow says Moo, the duck says Quack, the badger grieves & dies
no longer will the thought be true when I look at you out of his eyes

Kiss the Host

In the night out with the rapt kids who need to read you
my vertebrae are piano keys, take them, push them down
make a song with your clumsy hands, the four angels
are trumpeting through the trees, through the very sky
the planet cries. You tank your rest, think about yourself
take a friend over the shadowy bridge when the town's
collapsed, when the electrical plant explodes, traffic cops
walked off the job, lawyers jumped into the river
power wounds, all I want, I met a traumatized orphan
who pinched the name of some disastrous demigod
spreading around the line with a nouveau demimonde.
A strip of amber light lanterns up the horizon like
another neglected promise, awe with no payday.
I like your parties, I pray at the altar of wine, I
kiss the host! I do just fine, broken swans piddling
around the north side of the metropolitan jewels
stupid like you, covered in pitch and anarchy like you.
The courtier knows what to do with that ring
and when to bend over and when to sing.
Are you white, are you real, do you fasten the seal?
You might get killed in a war but the sorcerer said you deserved it.

Western Treasures

Deaf, half blind, shut off from his fellowmen
by his deformities the bells were the only voice
of his groping soul. In dreams he took the shape
of a mute horse with the head of a mantis and passed under
the instruments, looking into their mouths, too wounded
to feel anything but dickless longing. The world punched
him straight in his insect throat; he was as dysmorphic
and gorgeous as people and cities are, but we feared him.
His rouge tears fell from the clocher like affreux rain
and only inebriated mystics conjured secret knowledge
in the puddles they designed between the cobblestones
and only wacko unpersons used them as portals
to appetites and all the forgotten Western treasures.
Son, don't ask why the monster weeps, you don't want to know
he lives in alarm, means us every harm, and we call him Quasimodo.

When I was young and abused in my youth
my mother used to press her body against mine and tell me
"Take my strength" which, at the time, was enough
for me. I knew she could (give it). And if I, now, had a
super power, it would not be to gift but to receive
to absorb human misery
but in my doing so (really, how else am I to use it?)
not lessening the suffering of the subject
just duplicating it
secreting it away and aestheticizing it
so you'll never know what I took from you
but it was the part you most needed rid off
except I just made a copy of it, left the original in place
and cried over my witchery and that was poetry (?).

You are going to swing in denim from the towers
of the burning cathedral on the Île de la Cité
and if you can save me or redeem yourself...
well, do it.

Blond Villain

The state is so unsexy
An armored melody
Lashes out, hardest to
Explain—right at the end
Maybe, blondie, perpetuator
Presidents don't play
With our throats, lingering
Malfeasance, histories
Unyoked from intentions
Taunting and turbulent
Exquisite employment
Ordering principles are
Implicit in the argument
A vessel of erotic guilt
Secretarial in correlation
Upright spontaneously
The guitar is a bomb
The bomb is a shoe
The shoe is a phone
The phone is a knife
The knife is a gun
A gun is the best
Plump heads of state
Crossing the casino
Financing a coup
Drinking Mountain Dew
Want whom they will
And destroy the rest.

The bad guy cackles
And karate chops me
Down an elevator shaft.

I'm Funny

What choices are before me, it's a chore to discern
hardly been a minute since things were so much different
when your parents were kids they got away with a lot
they murdered loads of people and were never caught
I'm stuck, he stunk, mean boyfriends carving their
initials into a tree trunk, soused vandals—particularly
horned up about the next local election; democratic
erections chopping into the sky, that's a vista
and there's no chance in hell to get home on time
but we stopped caring about that binges ago
the lunching mountain troped out at the maximum
prohibition as an economic hoax, the jokes we tell
to get out from under the front wheel of the car
peppering the scene with an unfamiliar sense of hope
tantamount to reading fiction, tasting you again
out of nowhere, I can't wait till I don't remember
any of this—that usually happens around sunrise
perhaps I have followed threads proud and unwise
Walt Disney would turn your gay ass into the feds
so fast your beak would spin around your head
he'd testify that you suck cock and want to share
everything, which in this country is a high offense
I thought the deal was all we'd say is "I'm funny."

Songs About Men

You took me out to the field because you were a guy in a hat
played some straw round my coarsening opening hymns
me thought, *Well how could I not fall for a hunk like that?*
I loved the thought of you too much, thus spake my therapist
we both had pellucid minds and energetic souls, kissed in micro
broke as orange skies, we skateboarded trails of thick gloop
across the landscaped ornament of what we wanted to do
was it blood or was it what we tried to keep from our parents?
god was dad and we, jovial, drank dreams of Hollywood help
landing in dunked gutters glowing north of where the fun was
less than punk and covered in glass and piss, still kinda a minus
weren't we about to get natural? ever tossing une gross video
into a chosen grave, which was only loaned, yet still all ours
twas a narrowing space, and reeked of chain smoke and cum
I asked for your confidence and you handed me a broken pipe
you planned to play my butt like a Jew's harp, get over yourself
the wind had other ideas, we just fell out of touch as we touched
some governmental bureau got involved, then it was dirty
nobody wants to be one of those little fish skeletons, donning
a party that's far pearled out and you never loved me piggy
fingers ended up pointed, thoughts got wrecked in the sexy mud
we turned it into a play and strode the boards screaming
I used to be a person! I was a blameless infant dressed in pink!
landlord got suspicious because of the stink; we persevered
until the hot crack of night licked our radical orifices, not done
of bone, honey, and umbrage; we might as well have dodged
into another day where you, galoot, have eviscerated the stale
youth clean off of industrial good intentions (then we did heroin
and fell in love again) I strum the chest hairs, stood straight up
muy appreciation or hate scattered as glitter o'er the skull

it grew florets and spent the last of burgeoning succoring me
drafted into the early plastic of being secure, as I am today
a request for songs about men, wailing benignly into the soil
the effaced area, teeth reflected in miles of destroyed leather.
 At last we turned into these weird kind of copper figurines
that mourned in the middle of the city when it snowed hardest.

Christmas Day

I've been in the promiscuous land of starving horses
and other pictures of uncommon nature
half a year homeless
wasted the year before:
there was his hair, the color of praline
like the triumph of Christmas Day.
Behold the nudnik, clomping through the slush
toward the cemetery in his cache, galoshes of vulcanized rubber
my tongue was just getting used to our unknown pleasures
most of the men were asleep.
Regions of the dead and newly birthed
petting out portions in retribution for some long abandoned slight
saying finally there is nothing to confront, just me.
I'm over it:
I've struck my pen against a rock
held a baby and, in awe of his ponderous face, been gentle.
Let this city carve hollows of damage through our coursing souls
let the maniacs keep their historic appointments.
There is no machine left to call you
there is no future but what sullies the top of our heads
on a walk along another disorderly canal.
During this season all I know
is that there are ghosts that hang in the air
and that's joy.
I might as well call it that because, save loss, we're thinner
and more resolved;
and the whole world is turning colors as we wake up.

Shortest Book in the Bible

Hath he not reckoned us strangers?
For he hath sold us and devoured our money
Don't expect to get old: the years will slough off your skin
Like a timeless hypocrite
It gets too long and multitudes counteract their judgment
What cannot be given up exposes us
Makes us forget our business
Lunges skew
The memory of having been well and valuable
The place where the bad thing happened
Spoken about, cavalierly, or with a little zest in punishment
Thrown into an open field
Explode the starling!
I will follow an erstwhile lover through the dusky syllabary
Our hearts are bent toward hell
Though we'd rather discover the toilsome bridleway
Where is the power
The thing long foretold but never gotten around to
The mythologic commonalities of indexical heft
But amorphous genetic makeup, bleating answers
The ear of god is burning
It puts one into a tiny box and glamorizes the soma
We came in on the wrong horse and were ruined
Left to the floors of recent justice
Messages abound, taxed into the ground
And I'm left with my love for my friends

My friends: do not echo what is evil
But realize what is spread through with grace
Those who love, god loves
Those otherwise are far away from god and do not see

Coriolanus' Farewell

In the dawning hour I woke cradled in the arms of a Parisian twink
who glowered exigently into my face and said, "Ariel Sharon est mort."
It did not feel like anything, the world dreaming and devouring itself
curling like Marlboro smoke into the stale wallpaper
the shepherds bent down in their pastures
everybody looked the same closed in investment.
I've already quit all that, it happens without me
and I'll take my dearest leave
the tanks roar like warthogs in the distance
the drones buzz but as cicadas in spring
this is how the story has always gone, adieu to my mother and friends
it can be blamed on me accordingly
it can never be destroyed.
We have murdered each other while our children watched on
that is why I was born, tall and bumptious hearts feasting
on the sick blood of history
and I tried, and I held this awesome boy
but you wouldn't keep me there.
Every pestilence has landed upon our naked heads
and I am heading out
I go alone into the recesses of my own war
making a solace of my hazards.
More than seen, my wicked swamp is feared
like that of the lonely dragon.

Triangle for Aaron Swartz

"All those moments will be lost in time, like tears in rain."
—Rutger Hauer

The ringing blades of winter pass along the torrents and channels
of lengthy optimism yielding no purpose but their own sound
a power enough to set about barbering the trunk of mercy
shared from what frequency prolonging whose agony
we enfranchise the information turning on arbiters
the peace all sources put under understood to be
a radiance from which threshold a darkness
from what desire the observance since
inhalations and annihilations I'm
so sorry they did this to you
the long arm of the law
and other demons
enclosing in
a forever
no less
here.

Going Back for the Cat

Januaries rattle round my life like loose teeth in a skull
those begotten, forgotten, forgiven, betrayed, and allayed
there is one more thing that the devil failed to say:
I am not like you, I'm not staying on the ship, I am
going back for the cat. All elusive impulse, kneeling there
by the bed, you can present forever (but you can't).
I'm not surprised, not surprised, not surprised—wish
you would have thought of me sooner, Damocles eschewed
we swallow the sword, the string, and the thought of death.
Just to take it in the dunes, just to tell me, be obvious
how lucky to even have, how damned, how shaped in front
waggish crossings and small braids, defend the hopeful
kingdom, drive over the jinxed girl and smear her father.
Yes, there is beauty, I collect it in my greedy lungs
my hair is suffused with it, my spine is quaking from it
I don't know how I am going to get out of it, lest I burst
into atoms and pleasure—let's just leave it at all of that.
There is no repeating, disappear into the small trails
of the board of the lost and the years, guiltiness holes
itself into a sheath of warlike aspiration. Some new day
some sky, sometimes being complete with what is left.
I'm going to carry this without, until, and through love
go back, get off, stand in, outdoor, cruise, stare, prepare
it is all gone, then we shall see what, truly, trophies want.

Lost Metropolis

The children of the plague gave up on Manhattan
and crawled, half-alive, toward outer boroughs
wet flakes of snow dribbled across their shoulders
their scleras glowed neon, virescent in the dark.

The company called them valetudinary moochers
as they slopped us out of their cancerous wombs
into garbled ditches and patches of filth under bridges
we screamed our chosen names into the whorish night.

They stashed us in neglected apertures, stalked off
to die in the oncoming shadow of the entitled monolith
as the burning orb of a new century climbed the horizon
and our sallow eyeballs adjusted to such rancorous light.

Clearly we'd been marooned in an inimical region
where rawboned cats wept blood and absently fought
we took the rancid semen of abusers as our milk and
supped on chunks of pitch we'd plucked from the road.

There were those who dreamt of escape, some tried
some asked questions and others mindlessly survived
some flung their bodies in front of buses or trains
still others clawed vainly at the palace's skeletal gates.

Observers study us from the other side of the river
aghast or amused, it doesn't really matter to us
our mother is this wilderness and our father is pain
even if we could get out, we'd still come back again.

Valse Romantique

I'll never leave you like that
burbling profanity under the Porte Saint-Denis
fingering your icarian longing
nobody wants to admit it
jilt the name and tell me of all your marvelous ideas
and that your life is a sapid opera
the time to come is not waiting around anymore
it has got too easy to live
lights don't all communicate the same thing
massive as a church, twice as unrelenting
if we could just get a handle on it
chasing our own diegetic noises through the Marais
get it out, push it away profoundly
I am to you as the tops of cultivated trees in the blighted city
getting through to this could end up being a more troubling application
than we dreamed when we met
if we have met yet, if that was really you
and not a bunch of raccoons in a debonair three-piece
and listen—be sorry or farouche, but do not fink on love
it took a long time to develop these nodi, and they are in fact real
and'll continue to damage
even as we shake free of each other over sleights and parlor tricks
misremembered phrases and jabs, the telling of the cold
young and disabused, how many shapes
have I fallen for, idealized, loved
and how can you say how it has comminuted the will
planted a new letter
and strung again across the Seine
all the rues connected to Boulevard Voltaire
how am I supposed to respect you

how am I going to deal with the boys
meandering through my truth as they do
like a clowder of bored grimalkins
perhaps I'm soon to change my mind
dancing as I am along a declivity
pouting the news, giving up again
to respect, tired of antiquity
interrupting the eldritch holidays and paths
that we skipped to in the way of being apart
written for novel men imbuing scuppers and disowning the reason
how all things are cherished in their own right
and the failsafe of a different night seduces me through your temper
dawdling and cute like the grounds I abandoned in getting here
to this umbrageous position
under the cracking flares of prized nostalgia
where we flicker and jot and dissipate
into a terraformed atmosphere far away from the gamboling tribute
erstwhile lovers built along the course.

Flesh Rebels

The laws are different now, raddled legislators hem
and munch at the heels of their venal colluders
the sweet town and its haptic pleasures benched back
like this body, scumbled by the dull veil of affluenza
now to be the unswept ground beneath white strides
scabrous variations, things clogged with privation
and want of contact, the mountain devoured her
as customers, local detectives found the corpse
facedown in a sour tarn like a drunken bank
weeks later, after the festival, a dahlia in her throat
the king's son was sent away on courtly business
his mom took an injection and retreated to her closet
nobody wants to talk about it but they dug up graves
and put on the coin the faces of defeated ancestors
so pro, so analgesic: these fugacious tyrannies
a more disciplined weapon blotching futures
hang on your mussitation, clodpoll, bless and believe
for there is precious time to elaborate the engine.
Before the mind the flesh rebels, spurting into its
red eden, consuming as it shall be plethoric.

Useless to Love

How should my magic universe a benign eidolon
none faster, getting it through the committee
bells, no reverence, politely some sort of absolute
last light shrinking into the snow on the lake
somebody put him in a turret, sled lengthwise
he doth bestride the narrow world, in time
when he can, when met at the corner of his own
I am watching from the crag, crucified against
our rock, myrmidons all are we, taking the fix
I've seen you in many better youths, I longed
for disasters as complete as philosophy bears out
gently now and with a feigned remorse, tell me
how did we get to the verge of this citadel
how could we not have seen ourselves coming
over the purple horizon, trailing behind us the
shaken portrayals of imagined events and yen
I don't see this holding, though ensconced in
the grume of particulars and responsibility
we came up short and in fear, obsessed by
what we thought was right, set under spells
break it out, I don't care, turn around, actors
are smiling into pieces of light, can't do it
the fog rising from the top of your head
it's forgiven, makes no difference, but it is
like a tamer coyote breezing along the porch
eyes aflame in reflection of the claim service
if I did anything for you I'm sorry, if you
ever thought of me obligingly, I am so sorry

don't explain it—slap, slap—swiftly do away
with all that we have made and failed to make
my chest is just a killing field, yeah I'm
dramatic, it's almost the crowd, no animals
compete with the daughter's secrets, put it off
it's simply so useless to love, but we often
lack the imagination to do anything else.

Looking Away

Fuck you: sex and cigarettes
washing blood from the wound
I need compensation
for all the time
spent in hells of my own devising
I was amazed to learn then
that it wasn't all my fault
wonder if it was worth it
not sure by which measure to judge
but I have a stabbing suspicion
all that pain was for nothing again
and then there's what we did
can I obliterate it
when drunk under the stars
my words sprawling out in steam
a boy at my back
with a perfect mind
brazen in movement
but soon left behind
as headlights scream in our faces
I cannot regret the economy between us
don't remind me what was said
you already got me
looking away
throwing off
the felony of belief
it was me
sick in the afternoon
fucking you on a mattress on the floor

there's no way we'll get rid of each other
remember the time I lied
naked in celebration with you
singing a forgettable tune
worried about what next to do.

Roundelay

I found you there in your defenestration, inconstant and foxy
we gossiped and hunted for the temperate favor of the paraclete
we passed each other in circles, performing a wobbly roundelay
I fell out of step and watched you disappear into another gallery.

I followed you into the pensioner's building, older than our country
we pulled each other's garments off and I fit my mouth against yours
we squinted into the white glebe to make out a pretermitting effigy
I fell out of step and watched you disappear into another gallery.

I entered late to drink the marrow of your unemployable apology
we stood lax in the snow outside the gates of the locked garden
we chased our blanching love around the edges of last January
I fell out of step and watched you disappear into another gallery.

I defended all of our evaporating ideals with perfervid gibbosity
we walked through the guts of the structure, sharing cigarettes
we dreamed, skimble-skamble, of an apocryphal prophecy
I fell out of step and watched you disappear into another gallery.

Late Winter

We halt in the woods
midway through a difficult journey
and listen to the silence around us
as the horses stamp the snow
consider us queerly
wondering which way
we each will go
failing the other
and losing control.

The Country House

The aging plutocrat whinnies, clasping to the idea
that gives him power. No dainty caracole can redeem
you, rescue your leverage, for we're fruitful with
the moral courage of the rash animal, hearts loosed
amok in the teeming frost, crawling across the field
toward the country house. I shan't tarry by the
inglorious fountain, nor hide the monster in the barn
there is what you think you do with the camera
and then the invisible mechanism—and the truth.
So tell me if you live around here, if that's you
on the roof of a Victorian manse, having abandoned
the city, ready to work a plew's worth of asinine
terror into the shocked hills. Have not you noticed
that the night is descending from the periphery
have not you heard the antsy pleas of less confident
constituents, willing to pay witness to the future onslaught?
You can tie me to a chair, clobber me, demanding I spill
the thesis—I can't divulge what I never knew, sorry.
I want a divergent province, I don't want what I can't
get back, I want the kind of sacred knowledge it's best
to believe never existed, I don't want to submit to this
meaningless energy, I want to abjure my wanton vocation
and become human again, I don't want what I just said
I want it not to be over yet;
I wish we could beyond.

Acknowledgements

Thanks be to Gore Abrams, Rijard Bergeron, Felix Bernstein, Cammisa Buerhaus, Cecilia Corrigan, Samuel R. Delany, Andrew Durbin, Ben Fama, Jay Laubsher, Gregory Laynor, Richard Loranger, Brian Marrero, David McConnell, Lisa and Joe Rapchick, James Sherry, Robert Yerachmiel Sniderman, Jacob Steinberg, JK Tallon, Deborah Thomas, Edmund White, and Don Yorty.

Some poems from this collection have previously appeared in the publications *Anthology of Young US Poetry* (Ukraine), *Best American Experimental Writing 2016*, *Brooklyn Poets Anthology*, *Cityscapes 2.0*, *Evening Will Come*, *The Lifted Brow*, *Lit Hub*, *Truck*, *Wealth*, *The White Review*, and elsewhere.

First draft written January 2013–January 2014 in Paris, Île-de-France; Brooklyn, New York; and Salisbury, Connecticut.